THE
BUFFALO
SOLDIERS

African-American cavalrymen, nicknamed Buffalo Soldiers, ride into battle in the American West. The Buffalo Soldiers fought bravely to help the United States settle its western regions.

THE
BUFFALO
SOLDIERS

TRACY BARNETT

MASON CREST PUBLISHERS

Mason Crest Publishers
370 Reed Road
Broomall PA 19008
www.masoncrest.com

Copyright © 2003 by Mason Crest Publishers.
All rights reserved. Printed and bound in the
Hashemite Kingdom of Jordan.

First printing

1 3 5 7 9 8 6 4 2

Library of Congress Cataloging-in-Publication Data
on file at the Library of Congress

ISBN 1-59084-072-0

Publisher's note: many of the quotations in this book come from
original sources, and contain the spelling and grammatical
inconsistencies of the original text.

CONTENTS

Although the Buffalo Soldiers were looked down upon and maligned, the African-American soldiers were good fighters, as they proved at the battle of Beecher's Island, when they rescued a company of white soldiers from a Cheyenne attack.

THE BATTLE OF BEECHER'S ISLAND

THE MORNING SUN WAS LIGHTING UP PIKE'S PEAK WHEN CAPTAIN LOUIS CARPENTER saw the two horsemen riding in from the east. The men had ridden through the night to bring Carpenter grim news: a company of about 50 soldiers a few miles away was trapped on an island, surrounded by hundreds of Cheyenne warriors. The soldiers were untried **recruits** under the direction of Major George Forsyth, who had fought years before with Captain Carpenter in the Civil War. Running out of food and ammunition, worn out after several days of fighting, they were desperately outnumbered. Many were badly wounded.

These were the hunting grounds of the Cheyenne and the Oglala Sioux. It was dangerous territory for the white men who had made up their minds to make the land their own. And for the black soldiers who came West to protect them— like the men of Captain Carpenter's Company H—it was even more hostile.

No one knows for sure why the Plains Indians dubbed their African American foes "Buffalo Soldiers." Some historians believe it was for the buffalo collars some wore on their coats. Others say it was because they thought the black men's hair resembled the fur of the buffalo. But the soldiers of the Ninth and Tenth Cavalries knew that the buffalo was sacred to the Native Americans, and they wore the title with pride.

Forsyth's men had no battle experience. Many were fond of drinking and brawling. Even Forsyth, who was a seasoned *veteran*, had no experience fighting Native Americans. But the group had joined the armed forces eager to do battle against the Indians who had raided their neighbors, and they were confident of their fighting skills. As they set out for the wilderness, they had scornfully turned down an offer to be helped by a troop of black soldiers. Many *frontiersmen*, like their countrymen back east, were *racist*. They wanted nothing to do with people of any color other than white.

But if Carpenter and his men knew this, it made no difference to them. The troopers wasted no time in breaking camp, saddling up, and riding northward into the sagebrush to rescue Forsyth and his men. It was September 22, 1868, and Carpenter's troop of Buffalo Soldiers—the Indian nickname for the enlisted black men of the Ninth and Tenth Cavalries— was on the move.

A week before, a Cheyenne warrior had sat quietly in a teepee, purifying himself for the coming battle. Roman Nose

> Roman Nose was a great warrior who was both feared and revered in his time. Like many Native Americans, he was a spiritual and superstitious person. His belief in himself and his power led him to incredible victories.

was his name, and he was honored by many for his seemingly magical powers on the battlefield. Like many of his followers, he had vowed to stop the white intruders who were destroying the Indians' ancient way of life. But today, he feared for his life.

He believed his magic battle *medicine* was broken by one thing: eating food that had touched the white man's metal. The day before, he had shared a meal with a neighboring Sioux chief, whose wife had brought them dinner. Roman Nose didn't realize until later that she had used an iron fork to take it out of the pot.

But there was no time to finish the usual cleansing ceremony; his men were insisting that he come with them on the raid against Forsyth's men. With Roman Nose at the helm, they believed they could not lose.

By nightfall of September 23, Company H had covered 35 miles. They stopped for the night and headed off again at dawn. Twenty miles further into the wilderness, they encountered a dry riverbed and a grassy field. Suddenly they witnessed a strange and horrifying sight: dozens of Indian bodies lying on wooden platforms throughout the field. At the center of the platforms was a tipi, and inside it, the body of a dead warrior. The man was wrapped in a buffalo robe and lying on a platform. A ceremonial drum and a shield lay at his feet.

Only later did they find out they had gazed on the body of Roman Nose. His spine had been smashed by a bullet from the carbine of one of Forsyth's men. His magic had failed him.

But Forsyth was still surrounded by the Cheyenne, and the Buffalo Soldiers forged ahead.

After they had trekked 18 miles further into the wilderness, they finally found the battlefield. It was on an island, in the middle of the Arickaree River. Captain Carpenter and his trusted assistant, Private Ruben Waller, led the charge. Soon the remaining Indian warriors fled. Carpenter and his soldiers crossed over onto the island with a wagon of **hardtack**, coffee, and bacon for the starving men. The men burst into a loud cheer, and Carpenter threw his cap in the air and shouted. The badly wounded Forsyth gripped Carpenter's hand in gratitude.

But what a horrible sight and stench greeted the rescuers. Fifteen men were wounded, including Forsyth. He had been shot in the skull and in both legs. Maggots were eating away at his flesh. Six of his men had died, including the company's doctor, J. H. Mooers, and Forsyth's second in command, Lieutenant Frederick Beecher. All 50 of their horses had died and were rotting away. The men had long ago run out of food, and they were surviving on the rotting horseflesh.

In the history books of the victors, the battle would come to be known as the battle of Beecher's Island, after the white lieutenant who lost his life there. In the oral history of the native people who first lived on these lands, it was known as the Fight When Roman Nose Died. But no one refers to the battle as the Buffalo Soldiers' Rescue. The role they played in saving Forsyth and his recruits barely gets noted in most history books, if it's mentioned at all.

But though history may have forgotten the Buffalo Soldiers, these brave men would play an important role in U.S. history.

This studio photograph portrays the dignity and pride of a black soldier in the Civil War. African Americans were permitted to enlist in the Union Army in 1862, and about 180,000 did so. Although for the most part the achievements of African-American soldiers were overlooked, some did earn respect and promotion.

2

A NEW FRONTIER

AFTER THE END OF THE CIVIL WAR, THE NEWLY FREED SLAVES CHEERED FOR THEIR NEWFOUND liberty. Then they looked at each other and wondered what they would do next.

The freed slaves had few opportunities to improve their lives, and fewer opportunities to win the respect of their countrymen. Many became **sharecroppers**. They worked the lands of their former masters and saw very little change in their daily lives. Many moved to the cities to work in factories under backbreaking conditions. The defeated Southerners were resentful and sometimes violently racist. Black people were **segregated** from whites in schools, churches, businesses, hospitals, and restaurants. Some were beaten or **lynched** for crimes they didn't commit. Everywhere, the story was the same: America did not welcome these new citizens.

After the nation had settled the "slavery problem" through the Civil War, many leaders began to look westward to the frontier as the next big battleground. White settlers had begun to pour into the frontier, eager for a piece of land and a fresh start. But that land was already inhabited by the Native

Soldiers are required to serve out their entire term, and they can't change their minds without going through a long legal process. When a soldier leaves his post or his command without permission, it is considered desertion. Deserters can be arrested and sent to jail.

Americans, who did not want to leave. They fought back as the government removed them from their homes and pushed them further and further West. Sometimes the settlers paid with their lives. Far more often, the Indians were the ones who died.

Weary after five years of bloody civil war, few soldiers were ready to take on another war out West. So the government turned to the freed slaves as a new way to fill the Army's ranks.

In June of 1866, Congress passed a law allowing blacks to serve in the peacetime army. Six regiments of "colored" troops, as they were called, were formed. Two were cavalry units, meaning they fought on horseback. Four (later combined into two) were infantry, meaning they fought on foot. The Ninth and Tenth Cavalries, as mounted troops, saw the most action. They were cited for their courage many times.

Some black men turned to the military as a way to escape the oppression of the civilian society. They dreamed of a life of honor and adventure as uniformed members of the United States Armed Forces. They were promised a wage of only $13 a month—but that was more than many of them could make

☛ Crispus Attucks, one of the men killed in the Boston Massacre of 1770, was a symbol to black soldiers. His determination in the face of danger and discrimination inspired Americans of all races to fight for freedom from Great Britain.

in the other jobs that were available to them. Plus, the wages included food, clothing, and shelter.

This wasn't the first time African American soldiers had served America. In the Revolutionary War, a fiery freedom fighter and former slave named Crispus Attucks was one of the first to take a bullet during the Boston Massacre of 1770. And nearly a fifth of the soldiers during the War of 1812 were African Americans. About 180,000 black soldiers also fought during the Civil War, many with great distinction.

But in spite of their proud military history, African American soldiers were still unwelcome in the government's

🔥 The Emancipation Proclamation was a landmark decree for all African Americans. It stated that all the slaves in the rebellious states of the south would be freed, although it did permit slavery in the border states. After the end of the Civil War, however, slavery would be forever abolished in the United States.

eyes. A 1792 law stated that only "free, white male persons" could join the military. It wasn't until 1862, when Abraham Lincoln's Emancipation Proclamation reversed the ban on blacks in the military, that black soldiers began to be enlisted in earnest. And that practice wasn't caused by a new openness to blacks so much as by the self-interest of whites. U.S. leaders realized that the Confederates were going to kill many more Union soldiers before the war was over—and a good many white men could escape death if a large percentage of those soldiers were black. However, many officers refused to serve with black soldiers, doubting that they had the stamina, courage, or intelligence to fight.

Ironically, a people who had little freedom themselves were being called on to help take away the freedom of another people of color, the Native Americans. But the cultural differences between blacks and Indians were far greater than those that existed between the newly freed slaves and the whites they had lived with for generations. Most black people were convinced that the modern, "civilized" society of the time was the best and only reasonable way of life. The Indians were "savages" who must be taught to live the way white people did—or suffer the consequences. So the Buffalo Soldiers shouldered their guns in a grueling, three-decade-long campaign to remove the Native Americans from their lands.

But the black cavalrymen did far more than fight the Indians. They also helped to pave the way for the opening of the American West. They built roads and bridges and forts, and they mapped thousands of miles of uncharted wilderness. They protected settlers, collared **cattle rustlers** and horse thieves, and chased Mexican revolutionaries back across the border. They even protected Native Americans on the reservations from white raiders and thieves.

But the soldiers of the Ninth and Tenth Cavalries received constant reminders of their low rank. Their guns were often castoffs from white soldiers, and most of the horses were old and war-worn. Stationed at posts with white soldiers, the Buffalo Soldiers were often the only ones ordered to do the manual labor of constructing new buildings and roads. And sometimes, they were stationed in places where white soldiers would never be asked to live, such as the collection of fallen-in and abandoned old shacks that made up Fort Quitman, Texas, when they first arrived there. The common view of the day was that blacks were better suited for the South's unhealthy climate, where diseases like typhoid and malaria were common.

Even though they sometimes gave their lives for the settlers they were protecting, it was a thankless job. Many of these same settlers harassed and threatened the soldiers when they came into town for supplies or an evening of entertainment. In Texas, a sheriff shot a black Medal of Honor recipient in the back and killed him—but the sheriff went unpunished. And a Nebraskan who killed three black soldiers, including another

Medal of Honor winner, also got away with murder.

These black warriors served with dedication. Life in the frontier barracks and on the battle trails was brutal, and many soldiers deserted. But desertion rates among the black troopers was much lower than that of the whites. On average one out of every four white soldiers deserted. But one year, the Ninth Cavalry didn't have a single desertion.

Frederic Remington, a journalist who marched with the Buffalo Soldiers, spent a grueling week on a long trek with the soldiers through the rugged New Mexico countryside. Later he wrote, "Officers have often confessed to me that when they are on long and monotonous field service and are troubled with a depression of spirits, they have only to go about the campfires of the Negro soldier in order to be amused and cheered by the clever absurdities of the men."

They fought with great courage, and 20 were awarded the Congressional Medal of Honor for their bravery in battle. Their courage helped open the West to white settlers.

3

WESTWARD BOUND

TWO CIVIL WAR HEROES, EDWARD HATCH
AND BENJAMIN GRIERSON, WERE THE FIRST
colonels assigned to head the Ninth and Tenth Cavalries.
Both were soon to realize that they would be fighting two
battles: One was the battle they had been assigned to fight,
to open the West. The other was just as difficult—the battle
to protect their men against the discrimination that
surrounded them. Their soldiers' treatment ranged from
petty and annoying to life-threatening.

Hatch was assigned to headquarters in an abandoned
cotton-packing factory in Greenville, Louisiana. There he
was to recruit and train the soldiers of the Ninth Cavalry.
The facilities were hot and filthy, and the men had to cook

> 🐦 Brave and loyal black troops were an asset to the
> United States military—even if they were not always
> treated as such. Camp conditions for black soldiers
> were often less sanitary and safe than those used for
> other soldiers, making it all the more challenging for
> them to prepare for battle.

Benjamin Grierson was a most unlikely man to become the leader of the Tenth Cavalry. When he was only eight, he was kicked in the face by a horse and almost killed. The accident left him with a deathly fear of horses and a terrible scar on his face. But Grierson was a brave young man, and he overcame his fears to lead the Sixth Illinois Cavalry in the Civil War. He led a 16-day, 600-mile raid through the heart of the Confederate South, a feat that earned him national attention as a Civil War hero.

After the war, Grierson signed up to lead the brand-new Tenth Cavalry, a challenge many of his fellow officers rejected. Many didn't want to lead black soldiers because they didn't believe they could fight. But Grierson had fought alongside freed slaves during the Civil War and had seen their courage and intelligence. He said he would be proud to serve with the black soldiers, and for his entire career he fought for their equal treatment.

Grierson was a former music teacher, and he soon raised the money to buy musical instruments and start a regimental band. Many long evenings at the lonely frontier outposts were cheered by the lively tunes of that band.

their meals over open fires in the middle of a **cholera** epidemic. Nearly 30 died in three months.

Grierson headed for Fort Leavenworth, Kansas, where he and his forces didn't have it much better. His troops were forced to place their tents in the lowest, swampiest area. When troopers became ill with pneumonia, the post commander refused to let them move their quarters or even provide walkways so they could stay out of the mud. Many of them died.

Military leaders had mixed feelings about letting African Americans serve even as soldiers. The idea of making them

Edward Hatch was a distinguished officer who had risen to the rank of Major General by the end of the Civil War. After the war, as the size of the army was reduced, many high-ranking officers were given lower ranks. In 1866 Hatch was made a colonel, and placed in charge of a new regiment, the Ninth Cavalry. Hatch started organizing this new regiment of African-American soldiers during September 1866 in Greenville, Louisiana.

Unfortunately, there were few other white officers willing to train black soldiers, and prejudices of the time prevented African Americans from becoming officers. On 11 white officers had reported for duty with the Ninth Cavalry by the end of 1866. There were other problems as well. Many of the black soldiers had been slaves, and they could not read or write. They were forced to live in overcrowded, derelict barracks. Their uniforms and weapons were second-rate. Diseases like cholera struck the Ninth Cavalry's camp in the fall of 1866, killing many soldiers.

Despite this, by February 1867 Hatch had organized 12 companies of black soldiers. The company moved to Texas in the spring of 1867, then moved west, marking the start of more than two decades of continuous service on the frontier. The Ninth Cavalry spent much of its time protecting Native Americans in the Indian Territory from white settlers who wanted to move into the Indians' lands.

Colonel Hatch remained in command of the Ninth Cavalry until his death in 1889.

officers would be out of the question for more than a decade. Many soldiers, like the famous George Armstrong Custer, refused to serve with black soldiers, even if it meant having a lower rank. Hatch and Grierson, however, were strong defenders of their troops. They had been supporters of the **abolition movement** and fought in the Civil War to free the slaves.

General William Hoffman, Colonel Grierson's supervisor at Fort Leavenworth, had no use for black soldiers, and he went out of his way to make the members of the Tenth Cavalry miserable during its stay at Leavenworth. He was the one who commanded that they place their quarters in the swampy area, and he refused to let them move when they began getting sick. He made the black soldiers stay at least 10 to 15 yards away from the white troops at all times, and he harassed Grierson endlessly with petty complaints.

But Hatch and Grierson trained their men and headed west. The Ninth went to Comanche and Kiowa country in Texas, and the Tenth went to fight the Cheyenne throughout Kansas. Some of the Tenth Cavalry went to Indian Territory, the land that later became Oklahoma, to serve as peacekeepers. The government had set this land aside for the Native Americans, but white settlers known as "boomers" kept coming in and staking out the land for themselves.

Tribes like the Cheyenne had been promised that if they gave up their own land, the Indian Territory would be theirs forever. They were furious with the whites for coming in and

👆 Life in a military camp was hard for all soldiers, whether black or white. Soldiers could not always depend on clean water and supplies, and Indian raids were always a possibility.

A corporal in the Ninth Cavalry poses on his horse on the Lakota Sioux Pine Ridge Agency, South Dakota. During the last decades of the 19th century, African-American soldiers were directed to put down another oppressed minority: Native Americans.

stealing the little bit of land they had left. They felt justified in taking revenge on these settlers. Some Native Americans raided *stagecoaches*, trains, and homes, sometimes killing and stealing and burning.

The Plains Indians depended on the buffalo for their way of life. They used every part of the buffalo: its hide for their homes and their clothing; its sinews for thread; its bones for needles. But buffalo robes had become very popular among white Americans, and people like "Buffalo Bill" Cody began to make their living shooting scores of the giant beasts, taking the *hides* and leaving their carcasses rotting in the sun. Some train companies were offering special hunting package deals, and tourists from the eastern cities would buy a gun, don a cowboy hat, and fancy themselves great hunters as they shot scores of the gentle beasts from the train windows. The Indians knew that the buffalos' days were numbered, and that their lives were in danger of

For most African-American soldiers, the highest rank they could achieve was sergeant. Few blacks were allowed to become officers in the U.S. Army, so the Buffalo Soldiers were led by whites, for the most part. During the 19th century, only three African Americans graduated from the U.S. Military Academy at West Point and became officers in the army.

ending, as well. They felt they had no choice but to fight to sustain their families and their way of life. They declared an unwinnable war against the men who had killed their buffalo by the thousands.

Into this tense and violent situation rode the Buffalo Soldiers in the summer of 1867. Many of these young men were teenagers, like Emanuel Stance, who enlisted in the Ninth when he was barely 19. Many were former slaves. They probably had no idea of the struggles that awaited them: 100-mile marches under the blistering desert sun or freezing nights huddled around a fire on the high plains. Some were

Emanuel Stance, the first black man to be awarded the Congressional Medal of Honor, was a puzzling individual. He was a courageous soldier—many would say a hero. But he was also a drinker, a troublemaker, and apparently, a bully. It was probably these qualities that led to his mysterious death.

Stance was one of the first to join the brand-new Ninth Cavalry in 1866. He was only 19. He soon proved himself an able leader, and while stationed in Texas, he was assigned to lead a patrol that was seeking Apache horse thieves. He succeeded in his mission, risking his life several times in the process. His commanding officer, Captain Henry Carroll, was very impressed with his courage. Captain Carroll recommended him for the Medal of Honor, which Stance later received.

But Stance had a bad habit of getting into fights with his fellow soldiers. In 1872, when First Sergeant Henry Green reported him as drunk on duty, he got into a fight with Green and bit off part of his lip. Carroll defended Stance in several court marshals, and Stance got off with little or no punishment.

Stance was, however, demoted to private. Soon, after demonstrating his great courage and skill on the battlefield time and time again, he was promoted again to first sergeant. Unfortunately he bullied and tormented his men. On Christmas morning of 1887, he was found dead on the road near the post, shot in the back of the head with a revolver. His own soldiers, fed up with his brutal treatment, are believed to have killed him.

Civil War veterans, but most had never been trained for battle until they joined the Army. They certainly knew nothing of the **guerilla** tactics of the Plains Indians, who could mount surprise attacks and then melt away into the hills. But these recruits plunged right into battle on the plains.

Emanuel Stance was stationed at Fort McKavett in the middle of Apache country in central Texas when, in May of 1870, he made history. He was leading a band of 10 troopers on a scouting mission when he saw Apaches with a herd of stolen government horses. He formed his men in a line, and they charged the Indians, guns blazing, and drove them away. They gathered up the nine horses and proceeded onward, camping for the night at Kickapoo Springs. The next morning, on his way back to the Fort, he spied a party of warriors getting ready to attack a train. He and his men charged again, driving the warriors away, saving the train, and capturing five more horses.

The Indians were not about to give up that easily, though. They started following the troops and shooting at them. Stance wheeled around and ordered his men to open fire. The Apaches soon fled.

Stance returned triumphant to the base with 16 captured horses and no injuries to his men. His commanding officer, Captain Henry Carroll, was enthusiastic in his praise of Stance, noting that this was his fifth successful conflict with the Indians in two years. He recommended Stance for a Congressional Medal of Honor, and on June 20, 1870, Stance became the first black soldier to receive the award.

But he would not be the last.

A Seminole chief known as Grizzly Bear, drawn holding his rifle. When African Americans mingled with Indians, they produced children who were hard to classify. The Seminole Negroes used their intuition and incredible survival skills to become scouts for the U.S. Army.

THE SEMINOLE SCOUTS AND THE RED RIVER WAR

SOME OF THE MOST DARING, RUGGED, AND
SKILLFUL BUFFALO SOLDIERS WERE ACTUALLY
part Indian—Seminole Indian. These men were the children of
runaway slaves who had married Seminole Indians from
Florida to create a new people called the Seminole Negroes.
They were black as their African ancestors, yet gifted with the
wilderness skills of their Seminole forbearers.

They lived with the Seminoles in Florida for several
generations until the government decided to take away their
land in the 1830s. Then they were forced to leave their homes
and move to a reservation in the West.

This was before the Civil War, when slavery still was a way
of life in the South. Because they were black, the Seminole
Negroes feared they would be forced into slavery, and so a
band of them followed their leader, John Horse, across the

The Seminole scouts traveled in very small teams so they wouldn't attract attention. Often they were outnumbered five to one, but in the eight years of their heyday, not one was killed in battle.

border to Mexico where they could live in freedom.

There they joined the revolutionary army of General Antonio López de Santa Anna. The Seminole Negroes served Mexico well, and the Mexican government gave them a piece of land to make their homes.

But soon the Civil War in the United States came to an end, and the Seminole Negroes learned they could be free people once again in the land of their birth. They missed their friends and their families, and they heard that the U.S. Army wanted their skills. Their experience with the Mexican Army in the border regions had taught them much about the Lipans, the Apaches, the Kickapoos, and other tribes who raided Texas cattle ranches. Officers like Major Zenas Bliss had learned of their legendary tracking and fighting skills, and they recruited the Seminole Negroes to come and work as scouts for the 25th Infantry, one of the two all-black regiments. They were promised land and provisions for their labors, and so they came.

On July 4, 1870, John Horse once again led his people across the Rio Grande River. The Seminole Negroes had their own ways, and they hated the routines and rules of Army life. Rather than joining the Army, they worked out a deal. The scouts and their families would be able to camp on the base

John Hanks Alexander poses in military uniform. He was an 1887 graduate of West Point and served with the Buffalo Soldiers in the West.

in exchange for their services. They built Indian-style homes of mud and sticks with thatched roofs. Some of them went into battle in Indian headdresses decorated with buffalo horns. Even though the Seminole scouts never numbered more than 100 at a time, they soon became worth their weight in gold to the Army officers. They could spend months in the rugged desert countryside, living off the land—even eating rattlesnakes when there was no other food.

For about nine years the scouts worked for Lieutenant John Bullis, a red-haired, wiry man who was loyal to his men. Together they forayed many times across the Mexican border to track down and burn Indian villages and hideouts. Bullis's scouts admired him and accepted him as one of their own. He suffered the danger, the heat, and the hardship like the rest of

Members of the Ninth Cavalry prepare to mount their horses. Like other cavalrymen of the West, the Buffalo Soldiers had to be alert and ready at any time to be called to action.

his men. He treated the scouts like a big family, even performing a marriage ceremony for one of his scouts, James Perryman, who ended up marrying a captured chief's daughter named Teresita.

Meanwhile, the Kiowa, Cheyenne, Arapaho, and Comanche people had joined together in a revolt. They were tired of watching their women and children go hungry. The buffalo in the southwest were all dead, and the rations the government had promised were not being delivered. So they escaped the reservation and returned to their old hunting grounds in search of the few remaining buffalo. But settlers now lived on those lands. The angry Indians declared war, killing settlers, burning ranches, and ambushing stagecoaches. The Red River War had begun.

On September 20, 1874, a **battalion** led by a Captain Mackenzie rode up the bluffs to the Staked Plains, a high desert in West Texas and Eastern New Mexico. Four scouts went ahead of the troopers, including Adam Payne, a Seminole Negro, who was wearing a buffalo horn war bonnet. The four scouts met 25 Comanches, and they didn't hesitate. Payne jumped to the ground and shot the horse of a charging Comanche. He took on six warriors at a time, fighting them all off until the four scouts were able to break away.

The scouts continued on for many miles, leading Mackenzie to the Palo Duro Canyon on the Red River, the secret hideout and supply station for hundreds of warring Indians. On September 26, Mackenzie's men launched a surprise attack there. They were able to take the Indians by surprise and drive them away, taking 1,400 horses and supplies. With winter coming, this was a heavy blow to the Indians.

When they got back to the base, Mackenzie nominated Payne, along with seven white troopers, for a Medal of Honor. Payne was the first Seminole scout to receive one, but more of his fellow Seminoles would also be awarded the medal.

In April 1875, Bullis took off for the junction of the Pecos River and the Rio Grande. He had been assigned to find a party of Comanche horse thieves. He and his three scouts soon picked up the trail and followed it; finally, they crept up on a party of about 30 warriors.

They were outnumbered by more than seven to one, but they were fearless. Bullis fired into the group. In an instant, the Indians grabbed their rifles and responded with a hail of bullets. At last, Bullis ordered a retreat, and the scouts began to flee. But they looked back and saw that Bullis had lost his horse and was surrounded by warriors. The scouts rode back through the gunfire, shooting all the way. John Ward rode straight to Bullis, and Bullis jumped on the back of Ward's horse. Afterward, Bullis recommended that all three of his men receive the Medal of Honor.

Unfortunately, Seminole Negroes' amazing luck in the field and in battle didn't extend to their *civilian* life. Back at the *garrison*, the families of the scouts were having trouble with the neighboring settlers, who didn't like them and considered them outlaws. The Seminoles tried to get the government to give them the land it had promised them so their families could farm. But the government ignored their pleas.

One day a white man fired a gun into the Seminole camp on the edge of the garrison, killing one man and wounding another. The wounded man was 90-year-old John Horse. The Seminole Negroes were frightened and angered at the violence, and began talking of moving back to Mexico.

The officers they served tried to get the government to give the Seminole Negro families some land in the Indian Territory, but they were ignored. Even General Philip Sheridan, the man in charge of the U.S. Army in the West, pleaded with the government to give the Seminole Negroes land, but it never happened. Rations were given only to the scouts and the laundresses. The rest of the Seminole community had to make do with the vegetables they were able to raise in their small gardens and what little food the scouts could hunt or buy with their small wages.

The tensions kept building between the townspeople and the Seminole Negroes. On New Year's Day of 1877, just as Medal of Honor holder Adam Payne was ringing in the New Year, he was shot in the back and killed by a deputy sheriff who claimed Payne was wanted for knifing a black soldier.

Some of the scouts fled back to Mexico, where they felt safer. Others moved away to other parts of the country. Some became cowboys on neighboring ranches. A few continued on with the army, but in much smaller numbers.

Most scouts didn't get army *pensions* when the war was over. Even Medal of Honor heroes John Ward and Pompey Factor had to fight for years with the government to receive small pensions.

Meanwhile, across the West, the Buffalo Soldiers continued to fight for the white man's freedom to settle the frontier.

🐾 The Buffalo Soldiers played a crucial role in the long and difficult search for the Apache chief Victorio and his followers. They trailed the Apache band deep into unfamiliar territory in 1879 and 1880.

5
VICTORIO AND THE APACHE WARS

ONE MAN STOOD OUT AMONG ALL THE FOES OF THE NINTH AND TENTH CAVALRIES—A MAN who refused to live in the desolate desert reservation the government set aside for him and his people. Chief Victorio, the powerful leader of the Warm Springs Apaches, led the two battalions on a year-long chase that covered thousands of miles and tested the Buffalo Soldiers' tracking skills and endurance to their limits.

When the U.S. government had tried to force Victorio's people onto a reservation, he made his escape in August 1879 with an estimated 300 Apaches, including women, children, and old people. They quickly disappeared into the rocky, dangerous Black Range of southern New Mexico.

In order to feed his people, Victorio raided farms throughout the region, sometimes killing people. The newspapers published sensational reports of the murders. It was then that Colonel Edward Hatch and his Ninth Cavalry were assigned to track Victorio down—a job they hated. The

Much about the Apache chief Victorio is a mystery. Some say he was born to a Mexican family, stolen by raiding Apaches and adopted. Others say he was pure Apache, born of a long line of royal Apache ancestors.

By all accounts, Victorio was born to be a great leader. If he had been treated fairly, he would have been a strong force for peace. But he was betrayed by the government and the Army. Even though his people were driven from their beloved forests and mountains onto a hot, dry, and barren reservation, he resisted going to war for several years. But when he finally did hit the warpath, he led much of the highly trained and experienced U.S. Army on a year-long chase, tricking his pursuers time and time again.

Chief Victorio was a great guerilla fighter with piercing, deep-set eyes and long hair sprinkled with grey. He was 55 years old when he led the Buffalo Soldiers through the blazing deserts and rugged mountains of New Mexico, Arizona, and Texas.

Army officers considered him a genius and studied his tactics. His ability to attack and then slip away was especially surprising since he always traveled through the mountains with a band of women, children, and old people, whom he never abandoned.

troops were widely scattered across the Southwest, but Hatch mustered as many men as he could, and they fanned out in search of the Apaches. Soon Benjamin Grierson and the Tenth were called in on the search as well; the government seemed determined to make an example of Victorio, and thus end the Apache wars once and for all.

The long treks into the Arizona and New Mexico countryside were grueling. In just one year, 1879, Hatch's men logged almost 9,000 miles. The terrain was brutally difficult to travel—blistering desert sun and no water for miles on end; rocky canyons and cold, windy mountaintops; and a border with Mexico that Victorio would slip across just as the Buffalo Soldiers were on the verge of capturing him. Mexico had informed American troops that they were not to fight battles on its soil.

Benjamin Grierson's troops were the ones who drove Victorio back across the border for the last time. Grierson and his troops were in Texas at Fort Davis in July when they received word that 400 Mexican troops were close on Victorio's trail, and the Apaches seemed to be headed for the border near Eagle Springs, Texas. Grierson headed to Eagle Springs and set up camp.

Grierson was sleeping soundly when a loud thud outside his tent brought him to his feet. There lay an exhausted Lieutenant Henry Flipper, the first black officer in the United States. He had ridden 98 miles through the day and night to bring him the news: Victorio's men had been spotted crossing the border, and they were on their way. There was no time to lose.

Henry Ossian Flipper was born a slave, but he went on to become the first African American to graduate from West Point Academy, the leading college for military leaders. In 1877, he became the first—and for a long time, the only—black officer in the U.S. Army.

Lieutenant Flipper was an excellent soldier, well liked by most of his fellow officers. He served in the Victorio War and was praised by Colonel Benjamin Grierson as well as his captain, Nicholas Nolan.

Flipper was handsome, talented, and very well educated. Perhaps that's why he got into trouble. At Fort Davis, Texas, he befriended a young white woman, Miss Mollie Dwyer. They often went horseback riding together, but Lieutenant Charles Nordstrom, who had been close to Miss Dwyer before Flipper arrived, became jealous. Soon Flipper was arrested for stealing $3,791 from the post commissary. A court martial on June 30, 1882 declared him innocent of the theft but guilty of "conduct unbecoming an officer and a gentleman." He was dismissed from the Army. Grierson and other officers spoke out on Flipper's behalf, but Flipper was never allowed to rejoin the army.

Nevertheless, he led a very full and exciting life after his discharge. He became an engineer and a surveyor, a newspaper reporter, an author, an aide to a U.S. senator, and a translator. He spoke Spanish and traveled and worked in Mexico. He also helped develop the Alaskan railway system.

In 1976, schoolteacher Ray MacColl worked with Flipper's niece to finally get Flipper's dishonorable discharge overturned, 36 years after his death.

Grierson came up with a plan. He had his men surround every water hole and mountain pass they could find. Soon Victorio, desperate for water, came upon two companies of soldiers, stationed in Rattlesnake Canyon and ready for an ambush. Victorio sensed a trap, and he stopped. The troops opened fire, and the Apaches retreated; but they needed water, and soon they moved forward to attack. Grierson sent in two more troops, led by Captain Carpenter, and the Apaches fled with Carpenter on their heels.

The troops continued guarding the water holes for six days. Captain Nicholas Nolan finally led a company after them in hot pursuit right up to the Rio Grande. Victorio slipped across into Mexico and looked back at the United States for the last time.

On October 18, 1880, Victorio was killed by Mexican soldiers. His death brought peace along the border. There were still a few small bands of bitterly determined Apache warriors, but they were soon killed or captured. And while the Mexicans took the credit for the Apache defeat, it was the Buffalo Soldiers who had worn down Victorio, took his food and water, and driven him back across the border for his final battle.

The concept of the Ghost Dance came along at a time when Native Americans were feeling hopeless and betrayed. The emotionally charged ritual dance gave a refreshing sense of power and freedom to their increasingly controlled existence.

THE FINAL DAYS OF THE INDIAN WARS

THE WINTER OF 1888–89 WAS A GRIM ONE FOR THE SIOUX PEOPLE. MOST SIOUX WERE FEELING hopeless, miserable, and defeated. As for the Buffalo Soldiers and other troops, life was easier than ever. It seemed that the war was over.

One bright day in 1888 the sun began to darken. The white men called it an eclipse, but a Paiute from Nevada named Wovoka saw it as a sign. Feverish from pneumonia, Wovoka watched from his bed as the moon slowly covered the sun. Then he fell into a trance and had a vision that would give new life to Indian resistance.

Wovoka believed that God told him the suffering of his people was about to end. The buffalo would return, along with all the Indians who had died in battle. The Paiutes, the Sioux, the Apaches, the Cheyenne, and all the others who had once roamed free would be restored to their former glory. Wovoka was given a special ceremonial dance that the Indians were to perform. It came to be called the Ghost Dance, and Wovoka created a new religion to spread the news. Soon half of the 6,000 Sioux on the Pine Ridge and Rosebud reservations in South Dakota were performing the dance for hours on end.

The government agent on the Pine Ridge reservation was frightened. He began sending telegrams to Washington, begging for Army troops to keep the order. Soon the government sent 5,000 troops to the area. The first to respond were the Buffalo Soldiers.

When they saw the soldiers pouring into the reservations, the Sioux became afraid. Almost 3,000 fled into the Badlands. There they set up camps and continued the dance.

Soldiers began putting more and more pressure on the Indians in the Badlands to return to the reservation. They surrounded them and slowly drove them back to Pine Ridge. The Sioux, too cold and weary to resist, finally were pushed back to the reservation. One who escaped the Army's push was Chief Big Foot, who led a band of about 300 Sioux. Battalions from the Seventh and Ninth Cavalries went after them.

Four days into the manhunt, the Seventh Cavalry tracked down Big Foot and his weary, half-frozen tribe. Big Foot was so sick he was being carried on a travois, or a stretcher made of hides and poles. Colonel James A. Forsyth forced the bedraggled travelers to march to Wounded Knee Creek, where he surrounded their camp with hundreds of soldiers and four deadly Hotchkiss guns.

The next morning, soldiers searched all the teepees, taking about 40 mostly old and battered guns. Only one remained. A young Indian had hidden it under his robe; half-crazed with grief and anger, he fired into the troops, killing a soldier.

The soldiers let loose with a volley of bullets and turned the deadly cannons onto the camp, where the women and children were waiting. When it was over, nearly 300 Sioux were dead—two-thirds of them women and children—as well as 60 American soldiers who had mostly been killed by their own crossfire.

One of the inventions that helped speed the defeat of the Native Americans was the machine gun or automatic gun, such as the Gatling gun and the Hotchkiss gun. Hotchkiss guns were small cannons that sat on legs, and they spewed out a steady stream of exploding bullets.

Back at Pine Ridge, the Sioux who had returned from the Badlands listened to the echoing gunfire and feared the worst. When a messenger came back with the news, the furious warriors mounted their horses and headed for Wounded Knee.

That evening, Major Guy Henry, who was leading the Ninth Cavalry, got word of the massacre. After a long day of scouting, the troops jumped back into the saddle and rode all night, followed by their wagon train of supplies. They arrived at Pine Ridge at 5:30 A.M. and dismounted—but barely an hour later,

👆 A Ninth Cavalry trooper pauses to look for tracks during the Apache campaign in the New Mexico Territory.

Corporal William Wilson came riding up with the news that armed Sioux warriors surrounded the wagon train. The exhausted troops roused themselves and mounted their horses once again. After a brief skirmish, the warriors withdrew.

But the Buffalo Soldiers had barely lain down when they heard gunfire in the distance. Forsyth had been heading back with his men when he was ambushed in a narrow valley surrounded by bluffs. The Sioux were on the bluff tops, aiming their rifles at Forsyth's men. The Buffalo Soldiers climbed back into the saddles again and rode hard, reaching Forsyth's troops at noon. They took aim at the warriors, covering Forsyth's men as they made their escape.

In 30 hours, the Buffalo Soldiers had ridden for 22 hours over 102 miles of rugged countryside in the bitter cold—and had fought, and won, two battles.

It took two more weeks to round up the last of the warriors and force a surrender. When the last band of Sioux turned over their arms, an ancient era died and a new one began. The federal government declared the closing of the frontier that year, and the Old West became a thing of the past.

The troops packed up and return to their posts, except for the Buffalo Soldiers. They were ordered to stay camped in their tents throughout the bitter winter, just in case the Sioux should try one more time to fight for their freedom.

👆 Members of black volunteer units continued to fight for the United States after the Apache Wars. Once the frontier of America was considered safe, the Buffalo Soldiers moved on to help fight the Spanish-American War. It would not be until 1948 that the U.S. Army would be integrated, with black and white soldiers serving together.

THE BUFFALO SOLDIERS GO ABROAD

BY 1891, THE INDIAN WARS HAD COME TO A CLOSE. THE LAND FROM THE MISSISSIPPI TO the Pacific Coast and from the Canadian border to the Rio Grande River was now safe for the stream of westward-bound settlers. But the Buffalo Soldiers who remained with the military still had a few battles to fight before their chapter in history came to an end.

The Ninth and Tenth Cavalries were sent to Cuba, an island off the coast of Florida, in 1898. America had decided to join in the island's war for independence from Spain in what was called the Spanish-American War.

The Buffalo Soldiers continued to fight prejudice all the way there. One sign in a barbershop along the way south ordered the black soldiers to stay away. When the ship was docked in the harbor for several days, they were forced to stay on board the ship, while the white soldiers could come and go as they pleased. And when they set sail, the Buffalo Soldiers were segregated into the stifling and crowded area below deck. They were not given lightweight uniforms to wear in the hot tropical climate, like the other soldiers. Instead, they had to wear heavy woolen uniforms as they slogged through the steaming jungles.

Theodore Roosevelt, the second in command of the armed forces in Cuba, was in deep trouble. Somehow, he and his famous group of "Rough Riders" had lost their weapons, and now they were surrounded by heavily armed Spanish fighters. The Buffalo Soldiers marched in on both sides of Roosevelt's surrounded troops and, in a fierce burst of gunfire, drove the Spaniards away. Observers said the Rough Riders would have certainly died there in the jungle had it not been for the Buffalo Soldiers' rapid response.

And while every history book tells students about Teddy Roosevelt and his famous charge up San Juan Hill, very few even know that the man who cleared the way was a Buffalo Soldier by the name of Thomas Griffith. Crawling on his belly through the thick jungle undergrowth, he dodged bullets and cut barbed wire to make way for the Buffalo Soldiers of the Tenth Cavalry, who led that charge.

George Wanton was another Buffalo Soldier who should have made history during the Spanish-American War. He risked his life in a daring moonlight rescue, taking a small boat to shore to rescue several wounded men. He got them all out safely amid a rain of bullets.

👆 General John J. Pershing, who commanded American forces during World War I, had a great respect and admiration for the Buffalo Soldiers. This earned him the nickname "Black Jack" Pershing. The General trusted the commitment and competence of African-American soldiers.

In all, five black cavalrymen won the Congressional Medal of Honor for their bravery during the Spanish-American War. Twenty-nine of them died. Unfortunately, Roosevelt's gratitude didn't last long. The blustery war hero, who later became president, publicly insulted the black soldiers when he returned, telling newspaper reporters that they had been slow and cowardly. The record, however, denies his words.

While they were in Cuba, the soldiers of the Tenth Cavalry had served with a white officer who appreciated them far more than Roosevelt had. Lieutenant John J. Pershing admired their courage and their skill. When as a general 18 years later Pershing was assigned in 1916 to help track down the famous Mexican revolutionary Pancho Villa, he selected the Tenth Cavalry to fight with him in Mexico. There the troop spent a fruitless year riding thousands of miles through Mexican deserts and mountains until the American government, more concerned about the brewing World War I, lost interest. Pershing later was dubbed "Black Jack" because of his service with the Buffalo Soldiers—a distinction he wore with pride.

But the time of the horseback soldier had come to an end. Several black battalions fought in World War I, and the nation's first squadron of black fighter pilots distinguished themselves in World War II. In 1948, President Harry S. Truman ordered an end to segregation in the armed forces, and African Americans were integrated into the military.

Today a memorial to the Buffalo Soldiers' bravery stands in Fort Leavenworth, Kansas. Our nation's history would not have been the same without the courage and strength of these Americans.

GLOSSARY

Abolition movement
A pre-Civil War movement to end slavery in the United States.

Battalion
A group of military troops that are organized to act together.

Cattle rustlers
Thieves who stole cattle.

Cholera
A very contagious and often deadly disease that causes severe diarrhea.

Civilian
A person who is not in the military.

Frontiersman
A man who lived on the untamed edges of civilization.

Garrison
A military post where troops are stationed.

Guerilla
A style of warfare that involves hiding and surprising the enemy, instead of face-to-face fighting on the battlefield.

Hardtack
A hard, unsalted biscuit or flatbread.

Hide
The skin of a large animal, such as a buffalo or deer.

Lynch
To seize somebody accused of a crime and put them to death immediately, usually by hanging, without holding a fair trial.

Medicine

For Native Americans, the word has a much broader meaning than it does for other people. Medicine is something with spiritual or magical powers.

Pension

A fixed amount of money paid regularly to a person who has retired as a reward for service.

Racist

Believing that one race is superior to all others.

Recruit

A soldier who has recently joined the armed forces.

Segregated

Separated; in the case of black Americans before the Civil Rights Movement, black people were not allowed to use the same businesses or facilities as whites.

Sharecroppers

Tenant farmers who work a landowner's fields in return for a small share of the land's profits.

Stagecoaches

Horse-drawn carriages that were often used for travel and mail delivery in the West.

Veteran

Someone who has fought in a war.

TIMELINE

1862
On July 17, Congress approves enlistment of black soldiers to assist in the Union Army efforts in the Civil War.

1865
Confederate forces approve enlistment of African Americans on March 13

1866
Congress approves enlistment of African Americans in the regular peacetime army on July 17.

1866
In August, General Ulysses S. Grant telegraphs generals Philip Sheridan and William T. Sherman, commanding them each to create a regiment of black soldiers. The Ninth and Tenth Cavalries are created, and Civil War veterans Edward Hatch and Benjamin Grierson are placed in command. Later the 38th, 39th, 40th and 41st Colored Infantries are formed.

1868
Company H of the Tenth Cavalry, under Captain Louis Carpenter's command, rescues an embattled band of recruits under Major John Forsyth in the battle of Beecher's Island in September. Cheyenne leader Roman Nose is killed in the battle.

1869
The four black infantry units are combined into the 24th and the 25th Infantries.

1870
On June 20, Emanuel Stance becomes the first Buffalo Soldier to win a Congressional Medal of Honor for courage in battle; 19 other Buffalo Soldiers will also win this honor; the first Seminole Negroes return from Mexico on July 4, to serve as scouts for the 25th Infantry.

1877

On June 15, Henry O. Flipper becomes the first African American to graduate from the U.S. Military Academy at West Point. He is later appointed as the first black officer of the Tenth Cavalry.

1879

In the fall, Chief Victorio and 300 Apaches revolt, escaping from the San Carlos Reservation and beginning a series of raids. The Ninth Cavalry is assigned to New Mexico to lead a year-long hunt for the elusive Victorio in what later becomes known as the Victorio War.

1881

In July, Henry Flipper is accused of stealing $3,791 from the camp store, a charge that is later overturned by a federal court-marshal. Despite this, Flipper is dishonorably discharged from the military. Many of his fellow officers, including Benjamin Grierson, were outraged, calling the entire affair a case of discrimination.

1890

The Ninth Cavalry responds to an alarm from the Indian agent on the Pine Ridge reservation in South Dakota, in a conflict that will end the Indian Wars in the North.

1976

History teacher Ray MacColl works with the niece of Henry Flipper to appeal Flipper's dishonorable discharge. He succeeds in securing an honorable discharge for the former Buffalo Soldier 36 years after Flipper's death.

1992

The Buffalo Soldier Monument is dedicated at Fort Leavenworth, Kansas, on July 25.

FURTHER READING

Billington, Monroe Lee. *New Mexico's Buffalo Soldiers, 1866–1900.* Niwot: University of Colorado Press, 1991.

Cox, Clinton. *Forgotten Heroes: The Story of the Buffalo Soldiers.* New York: Scholastic Inc. 1993.

Kenner, Charles. *Black & White Together: Buffalo Soldiers and Officers of the Ninth Cavalry, 1867–1898.* Norman: University of Oklahoma Press, 1999.

Leckie, William H. *The Buffalo Soldiers: A Narrative of the Negro Cavalry in the West.* Norman, Oklahoma: University of Oklahoma Press, 1967.

Miller, Robert. *Buffalo Soldiers: The Story of Emanuel Stance.* Morristown, N.J.: Silver Press, Paramount Publishing, 1995.

Reef, Catherine. *Buffalo Soldiers.* New York: Twenty-first Century Books, 1993.

Roberts, David. *Once They Moved Like the Wind: Cochise, Geronimo, and the Apache Wars.* New York: Simon and Schuster, 1993.

Schubert, Frank N. *Black Valor: Buffalo Soldiers and the Medal of Honor, 1870–1898.* Wilmington, Del.: Scholarly Resources Books, 1997.

Schubert, Frank N. *On the Trail of the Buffalo Soldier: Biographies of African Americans in the U.S. Army, 1866–1917.* Wilmington, Del.: Scholarly Resources Books, 1995.

Stovall, TaRessa. *The Buffalo Soldiers.* Philadelphia: Chelsea House Publishers, 1997.

Yount, Lisa. *Frontier of Freedom: African Americans in the West.* New York: Facts on File, 1997.

INTERNET RESOURCES

The Buffalo Soldiers

http://www.zianet.com/wblase/courier/buffalo.htm

http://www.imh.org/imh/buf/buf2.html

http://www.coax.net/people/lwf/buffpage.htm

http://members.aol.com/roadk9/buffalo/soldiers.htm

http://www.ushist.com/buffalo-soldiers.htm

http://www.tpwd.state.tx.us/park/admin/buffalo/bf_history.htm

The Search for Victorio

http://www.buffalosoldier.net/BuffaloSoldiers&ChiefVictorio.htm

http://www.buffalosoldier.net/

http://www.tsha.utexas.edu/handbook/online/articles/view/VV/fvi3.html

Henry O. Flipper

http://www.dtic.mil/armylink/news/Feb1999/a19990223flipperf.html

http://www.army.mil/cmh-pg/topics/afam/flipper.htm

http://www.tsha.utexas.edu/handbook/online/articles/view/FF/ffl13.html

http://www.mobeetie.com/pages/flipper.htm

Seminole Negro Indian Scouts

http://www.buffalosoldier.net/SeminoleNegroIndianScouts.htm

http://www.coax.net/PEOPLE/lwf/scouts.htm

http://www.coax.net/people/lwf/sem_scts.htm

http://www.texancultures.utsa.edu/seminole/seminolescouts.htm

INDEX

PHOTO CREDITS

ABOUT THE AUTHOR

Tracy Barnett is a freelance journalist who has written for magazines and newspapers for 15 years. She has also taught writing and editing at the University of Missouri School of Journalism and is the founding editor of *Adelante*, a bilingual Spanish-English community newspaper in Missouri. She is translating a collection of Venezuelan stories for children. This is her first book for young people, but when she was 13, she began publishing a children's magazine called *Little Miss Muffet*.